THE STORY OF

Santa Claus

JOSEPH A. MCCULLOUGH

ILLUSTRATED BY PETER DENNIS

OSPREY ADVENTURES

First published in Great Britain in 2014 by Osprey Publishing,
PO Box 883, Oxford, OX1 9PL, UK
PO Box 3985, New York, NY 10185-3985, USA
E-mail: info@ospreypublishing.com

Osprey Publishing is part of the Osprey Group

A CIP catalogue record for this book is available from the British Library

Joseph A. McCullough has asserted his right under the Copyright, Designs and Patents Act, 1988,
to be identified as the Author of this Work.

ISBN: 978 1 4728 0342 9
e-book ISBN: 978 1 4728 0344 3
PDF ISBN: 978 1 472 80343 6

Typeset in Adobe Caslon Pro, Windsor BT and Birds of Paradise
Originated by PDQ Digital Media, Bungay, UK
Printed in the USA

14 15 16 17 18   11 10 9 8 7 6 5 4 3 2

Osprey Publishing is supporting the Woodland Trust, the UK's leading woodland conservation
charity, by funding the dedication of trees.

www.ospreypublishing.com

Contents

Introduction

Every year on Christmas Eve, Santa Claus visits millions of people all over the world, bringing presents and Christmas goodies and doing his best to spread peace and goodwill. With his red coat, white beard, sack full of presents, and magical reindeer and sleigh, he is one of the most famous and recognizable figures in the world today. Yet, despite his popularity, most people actually know very little about him. They might know that his original name was Nicholas, or Saint Nicholas, or that he was once a bishop a long time ago, but how did such a man become Santa Claus?

Even today, when he is loved by millions, Santa Claus remains a shy and quiet man. He rarely leaves the North Pole except on Christmas Eve, and only a few very lucky individuals have ever had the chance to visit him there. He has little interest in self-promotion, and values his fame only for the help it gives him in spreading Christmas cheer. Despite many requests, and several lucrative offers, he has never shared his full life story.

So to fully learn about this great man, it is necessary to collect all of the stories of the people who have known him, those who have had the chance to speak with him, and even the ones who have just seen him from afar. From ancient writers to modern poets, this book collects many of those stories and combines them into a simple tale that can be read and enjoyed by everyone. It is a strange and mysterious story, filled with prayers and miracles and even a few monsters. For some people, it will be hard to believe. However, for those who can keep an open mind and, more importantly, an open heart, they will probably discover that the full tale of Santa Claus is even more magical than they ever suspected.

CHAPTER I

Nicholas, Bishop of Myra

The story of Santa Claus begins nearly seventeen hundred years ago in the town of Patara in the modern country of Turkey. At that time, Patara was a part of the vast Roman Empire that stretched from Britain in the east all the way to Syria in the west. Despite its size and power, however, the empire was often a dangerous and unstable place. Barbarians and pirates raided along the borders, while Roman generals and senators plotted against each other in an effort to become the next emperor. Even among the common townsfolk there was tension between the citizens who worshiped the old Roman gods and the growing minority that followed the teachings of Jesus Christ.

Thankfully, being a small and generally unimportant town on the Mediterranean coast, Patara had so far escaped most of the troubles of the empire, and even the Christians and the other Romans tended to get along. Thus it was a happy day in the town when, around the year AD 280, a young Christian couple named Theophanes and Joanna were married in the small church. Both came from wealthy and noble families, and both had lived lives of generosity, kindness, and prayer.

Less than a year after the marriage, Joanna gave birth to a boy. They called the boy "Nicholas", a very unusual name at that time. It meant "people's victor," and Theophanes and Joanna hoped that one day their son might help the common people overcome the greed and corruption of the men who ran the empire.

As Nicholas grew up in that house filled with love and prayer, he soon showed himself to be an unusual child. He took little interest in material things. Toys and rich foods couldn't hold his attention, and he shied away from traditional entertainments such as dancing and drama. Instead, he found the most pleasure in quiet reflection and in hearing the stories of old Christian holy men. Stranger still, when Nicholas learned to talk, he often spoke about events before they happened, predicting the weather, or visitors, or even deaths and births in the town.

As Nicholas grew older, this ability also grew, but despite this power Nicholas never used his foreknowledge for personal gain. In fact, he avoided the markets as much as possible and shunned all involvement in politics. Still, he followed his parents' example in extending Christian kindness and proved generous with both his money and his time.

Then, when Nicholas was fourteen, tragedy struck. A deadly plague swept through the region, decimating the towns and villages.

Even the quiet town of Patara could not escape the disease. Hundreds died, including Theophanes and Joanna. Nicholas was left alone, a young and wealthy orphan.

THE FIRST GIFT

With his parents gone on to heaven, Nicholas decided to give away all his wealth and leave Patara. He would seek out a quiet and holy life somewhere else. But as he made his preparations to leave, Nicholas learned that one of his neighbors, a good man with three grown daughters, had fallen on hard times. In fact, the family had become so poor that they could rarely afford to eat. Nicholas realized that unless something changed, the desperate man would sell his daughters into servitude to keep them from starving.

That night, as the bright stars shone down on the rooftops of Patara, Nicholas took some of the gold left by his parents and put it in a leather purse. Then, wrapping himself in a cloak to hide his identity, he went out onto the quiet and deserted streets. Soon, he came to the house of his poor neighbor. It was dark and silent, and Nicholas knew that everyone inside was asleep. Taking one last look around to make sure he was alone, Nicholas tossed the purse of gold coins through an open window. With a soft clink of gold, the purse landed in a shoe. Then, pulling the hood of the cloak tighter around his face, Nicholas turned and walked off into the night.

The next morning, the poor man discovered the gold in his shoe. Astonished, the man gave thanks to God for the miracle. The money proved just enough to provide an attractive dowry for the man's eldest daughter, and only a few weeks later, she was married into a good family and would never have to worry about starving again.

When Nicholas saw the good that had come from his parents' money, he decided to make a second night time visit. Again he gathered some gold coins into a purse, and again he snuck out in the middle of the night when everyone else was asleep. This time, when he tossed the purse through the window, it landed in a sock that had been left by the fire to dry.

When the poor man found this second purse of gold, he again gave thanks to God. With this money, he arranged the marriage of his second daughter and secured a good future for her with a respectable family.

Although Nicholas had already delayed his departure from Patara for longer than he had intended, he knew he had one more midnight visit to make. So, a couple of weeks later, he dressed in his cloak, took the last of his parents' gold, which was twice as much as he had given before, and quietly made his way to the house of his neighbor. This time, however, when he threw the gold through the window, the poor man inside was awake and watching.

When he saw the purse land on his floor, he ran outside to see who had thrown it. As he reached the street, he saw a cloaked figure turn and run off. The poor man chased Nicholas through the streets and eventually caught up with him. When Nicholas turned around to face the man, his hood fell back. The poor man recognized his young neighbor and fell at his feet, crying tears of happiness and thanking Nicholas for his kindness and generosity.

Nicholas knelt down and gently pulled the man back to his feet. Then, he made the man promise that he would not tell anyone about the gold, or from where it came, until after Nicholas had died. It is only because that poor man went on to live such a long and happy life that the story is known today.

THE BOY BISHOP

No one knows exactly where Nicholas went after he gave away all of his money. Some say that he journeyed to the Holy Land and visited the tomb of Jesus and the site where he was crucified. Others say that he traveled around closer to home, doing good deeds and helping those in need. Either way, he eventually arrived in the city of Myra, down the Turkish coast from his home of Patara.

Although Nicholas didn't know it, he reached the city just a short time after the old Bishop of Myra had died. For days, the Christians in the town had been looking for someone to take his place, but being a bishop was a hard and dangerous job in those days, and no one around had the courage to accept the position. So the Christians had called upon the bishops of neighboring cities to come and help.

When the bishops arrived, they too searched for someone to take on the job, but they also failed.

Then one night, the most senior of the bishops heard the voice of God while he was praying, and God said to him, "Go to the church at night and stand at the entrance. Wait for the one who will try to enter secretly. Then take hold of him. He will be your new bishop. His name is Nicholas."

The senior bishop immediately ran and told the other bishops what he had heard. Although the other bishops were skeptical, they had run out of other ideas, so they went to the door of the church and stood watch.

Just as the sun began to rise the next morning, Nicholas walked up to the church. He had his cloak pulled down over his face, so that he might enter without being recognized. When the bishops saw him coming, one stepped in front of him and took hold of his arm.

"What is your name, my child?" asked the bishop.

"My name is Nicholas, and I am your servant," replied Nicholas, as politely as he could.

"Please, come with me," said the bishop.

The bishop led Nicholas inside the church, where many of the Christians of Myra had come for morning prayers. The bishop stepped in front of the people with Nicholas beside him, and then he spoke.

"People of Myra, your prayers have been answered. This is Nicholas, who has declared himself the servant of the church. He is your new bishop!"

THE GREAT FAMINE

Despite his unusual and unexpected appointment as bishop, Nicholas quickly proved himself worthy of the job. Every day he held mass for the citizens of Myra, teaching them of the life and miracles of Jesus Christ and demonstrating how to live a life of good works and charity. Soon he was recognized all over the city as a champion of the poor and oppressed. He collected food and money from those who could afford it and distributed it to those in need. He also became a man of justice, unafraid to argue the case of the common people against the wealthy and powerful who often tried to cheat them.

Then, several years after he had become bishop, a great famine settled on the country. Crops failed and people went hungry. Nicholas did his best to share what food could be found and take it where it was most needed, but as the weeks and months passed the situation grew increasingly desperate. Still, Nicholas held strong in his faith, and one day, as he was out offering help and encouragement, word reached him that a fleet of ships carrying grain from Alexandria to Constantinople had sailed into the harbor.

Wasting no time, Nicholas rushed down to the water where he found the captains of the grain ships. Nicholas immediately offered to buy a portion of their grain, but the captains refused. They said that the grain had been precisely measured in Alexandria and if they arrived in Constantinople with anything less than the full amount, they would face serious consequences.

"So you would let your brothers and sisters starve?" asked Nicholas. "Your sons and daughters? Look into your hearts and you will know what is right."

After that the captains talked it over amongst themselves and agreed to unload just enough grain to see the starving people of Myra through the crisis. They gave the grain to Nicholas so that he could divide it fairly and make sure that it went where it was most needed. Then the captains sailed away to face their fate.

When the grain ships finally reached Constantinople a miracle occurred. When each of the captains took his grain to be measured, he discovered that he had exactly the same amount as when he had left Alexandria.

THE TEMPLE OF ARTEMIS

After the great famine, the years passed quietly in Myra. Nicholas carried on his work as bishop, preaching and praying, but also helping the citizens with their worldly needs. Over the years, more and more Romans gave up their old gods and decided to follow Nicholas on the path of Christianity.

Then, one day, the great temple of Artemis, once the focal point of the city, gave a horrible groan and collapsed in a shower of broken stone. The crash could be heard all through the city, and a great cloud of dust rose up in the air until it was slowly blown away on the wind.

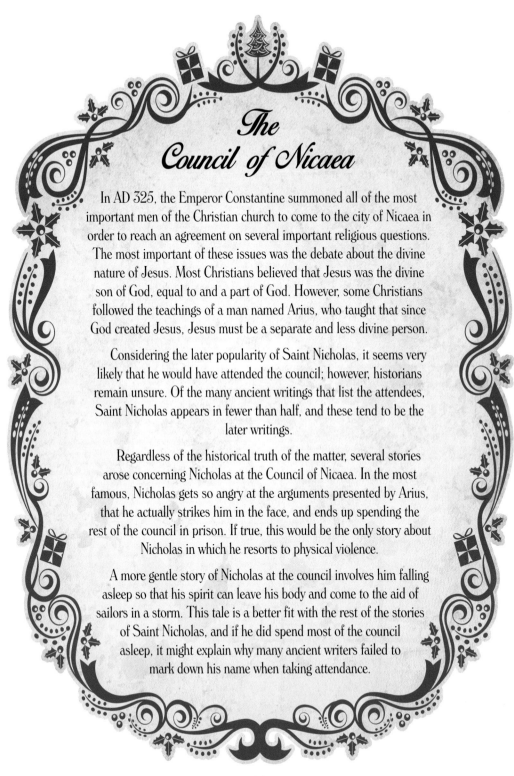

The Council of Nicaea

In AD 325, the Emperor Constantine summoned all of the most important men of the Christian church to come to the city of Nicaea in order to reach an agreement on several important religious questions. The most important of these issues was the debate about the divine nature of Jesus. Most Christians believed that Jesus was the divine son of God, equal to and a part of God. However, some Christians followed the teachings of a man named Arius, who taught that since God created Jesus, Jesus must be a separate and less divine person.

Considering the later popularity of Saint Nicholas, it seems very likely that he would have attended the council; however, historians remain unsure. Of the many ancient writings that list the attendees, Saint Nicholas appears in fewer than half, and these tend to be the later writings.

Regardless of the historical truth of the matter, several stories arose concerning Nicholas at the Council of Nicaea. In the most famous, Nicholas gets so angry at the arguments presented by Arius, that he actually strikes him in the face, and ends up spending the rest of the council in prison. If true, this would be the only story about Nicholas in which he resorts to physical violence.

A more gentle story of Nicholas at the council involves him falling asleep so that his spirit can leave his body and come to the aid of sailors in a storm. This tale is a better fit with the rest of the stories of Saint Nicholas, and if he did spend most of the council asleep, it might explain why many ancient writers failed to mark down his name when taking attendance.

Many people claimed that Nicholas had battled with the demon-goddess, Artemis herself, and cast her out of the city. Others said that the temple had collapsed through sheer neglect, as Artemis had so few followers left in the city. Nicholas himself said nothing on the subject but continued to concentrate on the needs of his own church.

And so the years carried on, and Nicholas grew older. Age lines appeared on his face, and his hair and long beard turned a snowy white.

THE PROVINCIAL GOVERNOR

Despite his advancing age, Nicholas remained full of youthful energy and continued his work amongst the people. One stormy day, an armada of ships came into Myra's harbor. The ships carried a Roman army, led by three generals named Nepotian, Ursus, and Apilion. The army was traveling to a distant corner of the empire in order to put down a rebellion, but had been forced into the harbor by the storms.

When Nicholas heard of the army's arrival, he invited the three generals to dine with him. This was not the first Roman army to pass through the city, and Nicholas wanted to make sure that the soldiers did not cause problems. In the past, soldiers had been responsible for thefts, fighting and worse.

Just as Nicholas and the generals sat down to dinner, a messenger arrived, out of breath from having run so quickly. He told Nicholas that Eustathius, the provincial governor, had condemned three men to death without trial and had already sent them to the place of execution. Wasting no time, Nicholas put aside his dinner, grabbed his cloak, and asked the generals to accompany him as he dashed out the door. Together the men hurried through the city until they reached the place of execution. They arrived to find three men, bound hand and foot with sacks over their heads, kneeling on the ground. The executioner stood behind them, his sharp sword raised above his head.

Nicholas pushed his way through the gathered crowd and yanked the sword from the hands of the surprised executioner. He used the sword to cut the bonds of the prisoners; then he cast the blade aside.

Still filled with righteous anger, Nicholas turned and marched to the house of Eustathius, followed by the three generals. When he reached the house, he banged on the door until it splintered and fell open. Nicholas stepped into the house and spied Eustathius cowering in a corner. The provincial governor greeted the bishop with stammered compliments, but Nicholas interrupted him.

"You dare to stand before me!" roared Nicholas to the trembling governor. "You are an enemy of God. A man who perverts the law for his own gain and sends innocent men to their deaths."

Eustathius fell to his knees before Nicholas and confessed his crime. He admitted that he had accepted a bribe to execute the three men, but pleaded that he truly regretted the decision. He begged for mercy and forgiveness.

Nicholas loomed over the man, and he looked deep into his soul, searching for the good and evil that dwelt within. He saw that the man was truly sorry for the mistake he had made, and that he was still a good man underneath. The anger drained out of Nicholas. He forgave Eustathius, and said a prayer and a blessing over the governor.

The three generals, amazed by everything they had seen, returned to their ships that evening. The next morning the storm had broken, and the army sailed away.

THE THREE GENERALS

Nepotian, Ursus, and Apilion eventually reached the site of the rebellion and, through careful negotiation, were able to end the uprising without bloodshed. The three generals then returned to Constantinople, where they were welcomed back as heroes. Emperor Constantine himself threw a grand reception in their honor.

However, a few men within the imperial court grew jealous of the attention paid to the generals, and they plotted against them. They bribed the imperial prefect, who went to Constantine and accused the generals of treason. He said that the generals had made a deal with the rebels to overthrow the emperor.

When Constantine heard the story, he grew livid, and his rage blinded him to the truth. He ordered his soldiers to arrest the generals and cast them into the dungeons. He would execute them in the morning.

A short time later, the soldiers hauled Nepotian, Ursus, and Apilion out of their beds, marched them to the prison, and locked them in a dark cell. As the jailor turned the key on their cell door, he told the generals of their impending execution.

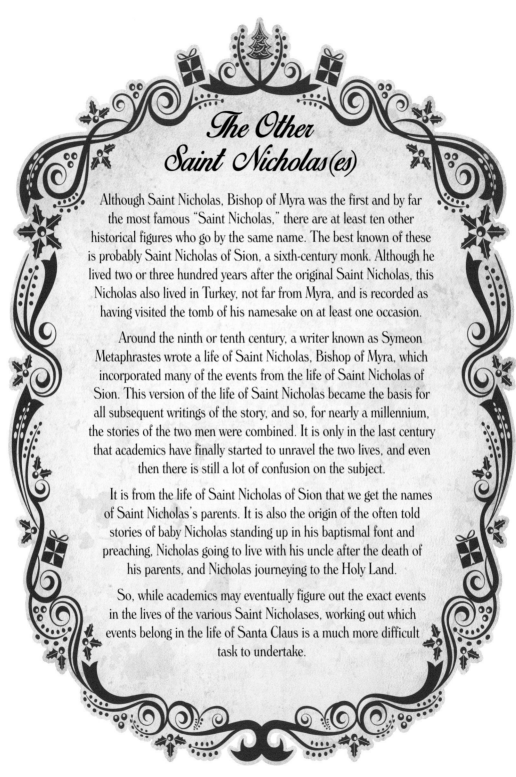

The Other Saint Nicholas(es)

Although Saint Nicholas, Bishop of Myra was the first and by far the most famous "Saint Nicholas," there are at least ten other historical figures who go by the same name. The best known of these is probably Saint Nicholas of Sion, a sixth-century monk. Although he lived two or three hundred years after the original Saint Nicholas, this Nicholas also lived in Turkey, not far from Myra, and is recorded as having visited the tomb of his namesake on at least one occasion.

Around the ninth or tenth century, a writer known as Symeon Metaphrastes wrote a life of Saint Nicholas, Bishop of Myra, which incorporated many of the events from the life of Saint Nicholas of Sion. This version of the life of Saint Nicholas became the basis for all subsequent writings of the story, and so, for nearly a millennium, the stories of the two men were combined. It is only in the last century that academics have finally started to unravel the two lives, and even then there is still a lot of confusion on the subject.

It is from the life of Saint Nicholas of Sion that we get the names of Saint Nicholas's parents. It is also the origin of the often told stories of baby Nicholas standing up in his baptismal font and preaching, Nicholas going to live with his uncle after the death of his parents, and Nicholas journeying to the Holy Land.

So, while academics may eventually figure out the exact events in the lives of the various Saint Nicholases, working out which events belong in the life of Santa Claus is a much more difficult task to undertake.

Bewildered and afraid, the generals tore at their robes and cried out their innocence, but no one listened. Then, after the initial shock had passed, Nepotian remembered Nicholas, Bishop of Myra, and how he had saved three other prisoners who had been falsely accused. He turned to Ursus and Apilion and grabbed their hands. He encouraged them both to call upon Nicholas for help.

That night while Emperor Constantine was sleeping, he had a dream that a white-haired old man came before him. The man pointed a bishop's crook at the emperor and spoke.

"Why have you arrested three innocent men and condemned them to death without proof or trial? Awake immediately and set them free. If you do not, I will send war upon your empire, and the bodies of you and your soldiers will become food for dogs and vultures. I have spoken with Christ, who is the king of kings."

Constantine, shaking in his sleep, responded, "Who are you to come and speak to me in this way?"

"I am Nicholas, Bishop of Myra."

With that, Constantine awoke as the light of dawn came in through his window. As he hurriedly got dressed, the imperial prefect burst into his chambers. The prefect had also spoken with Nicholas in a dream and demanded that the generals be released.

Wasting no time, Constantine sent his soldiers to halt the execution and bring the generals to the imperial court. When they arrived, the emperor stared at them long and hard, and asked, "Are you sorcerers?"

Nepotian, Ursus, and Apilion stared back at the emperor in confusion.

"My emperor," said Nepotian, "we have no knowledge of sorcery, but we have always been faithful to you and to the empire."

Then Constantine asked, "Do you know a man named Nicholas, who is bishop in the city of Myra?"

When the generals heard that name, they raised their hands to heaven and gave thanks to God. They told the emperor of their visit to Myra, of their meeting with Nicholas, and of all the great stories they had heard about the bishop.

Constantine, convinced by the truth of his dream, released the three generals. Then he gave them a new mission. He asked them to take gifts of gold and silver to Nicholas in thanks for his help.

The generals did as the emperor had requested. They returned to Myra and told their story to Nicholas. The old bishop smiled, gave thanks to God, and said nothing more on the subject. He accepted the gifts of gold and silver; then he gave them all away to those in need.

The Storm Tossed Ship

One day a great storm blew up in the Mediterranean Sea, forcing all of the ships to run for cover. One poor ship, however, got caught in the mighty winds and crashing waves, which tossed her crew about the deck and threatened to tear the sail from her mast. The sailors, drenched and terrified, clung on for dear life and called out to God to save them. Suddenly a man appeared before them, with a white beard and simple clothes.

The man commanded the sailors to rise up and see to their ship. Then he helped them with the sails and rigging and kept the

ship from keeling over or floundering in the waves. Eventually the storm died away. The sailors dropped to the deck in exhaustion, knowing that the stranger had saved their lives, but when they looked around for him, he had vanished from the ship.

Eventually the ship made safe harbor, and the sailors decided to go to the church at Myra and give thanks to God for saving them. When they reached the church, they met Bishop Nicholas and recognized him as the man who had been on their ship. The sailors fell to their knees and offered their thanks to the aged bishop. Nicholas smiled and told the sailors to give all of their thanks to God, for it was his power that had saved them.

When the sailors left the church, they told their tale to all who would listen, and in turn the people of Myra told all of the other stories of Nicholas to them. When the sailors eventually sailed away from Myra, they took the tales of Nicholas with them. They told his stories all across the Mediterranean Sea, and Nicholas became famous from one end of the Roman Empire to the other.

THE DEATH OF NICHOLAS

Despite his growing fame, Nicholas carried on serving the people of Myra, year after year, as his white beard grew longer and his tired back bent forward. Then, one day, he heard the voice of God calling to him and he knew that this chapter in his life had come to a close. He laid his weary body down upon his bed and prayed that God would send his angels to accompany him on his way. When he saw the angels descending, he closed his eyes and spoke.

"Into your hands, O Lord, I commend my spirit."

Then Nicholas breathed forth his soul and departed his earthly body.

CHAPTER 2

Saint Nicholas, The Wonderworker

After Nicholas died, his fame spread even more, and the stories of his faith, kindness, generosity, and miracles were told again and again. People started to call him "Saint" Nicholas because of his holiness, and they prayed to him when they were in trouble, asking for his intercession with God. Sailors prayed to him in rough weather because they remembered how he had saved the sailors in the storm. Prisoners called to him because they remembered how he had saved those who had been unjustly accused, but mostly parents prayed to him to protect their children for they remembered how he had saved the poor man from selling his daughters into servitude. Although Nicholas had passed on to heaven, he could hear the prayers of the people, and his heart still burned with a desire to help them.

The Lost Child and the Two Cups

Some years after the death of Nicholas, a nobleman visited his tomb in Myra to pray for a son. The man and his wife had tried for many years for children, but without success. The man promised that if he should have a son, he would order a golden cup to be made and would place it on the tomb of Nicholas.

Later that year, after the nobleman returned home, his wife became pregnant and gave birth to a son. Remembering his promise, he ordered a goldsmith to make him a cup of outstanding beauty. It took the goldsmith over a year to complete the project, and when the nobleman saw the finished work, his heart filled with greed and desire. He decided to keep the cup for himself and have a second one made for Saint Nicholas. Again he put the goldsmith to work, and more time passed as the smith labored to make a second cup as beautiful as the first.

Sometime after the second cup was finished, the nobleman arranged passage on a ship for himself and his son to Myra, so that they could place the cup on the tomb. During the voyage, the nobleman asked his son to take the first cup and fill it with water. The young boy misunderstood his father. Instead of filling the cup from the water barrel, he tried to reach over the side of the ship and get water from the sea. Tragically, the boy slipped on the wet deck and, still clinging to the golden cup,

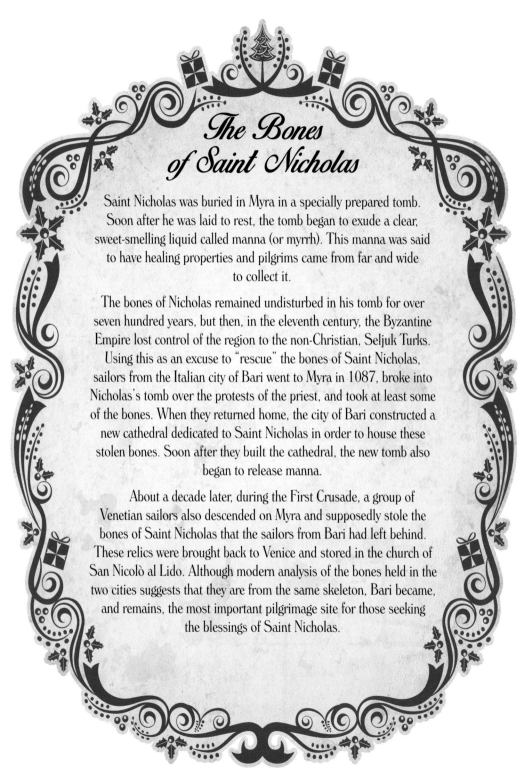

The Bones of Saint Nicholas

Saint Nicholas was buried in Myra in a specially prepared tomb. Soon after he was laid to rest, the tomb began to exude a clear, sweet-smelling liquid called manna (or myrrh). This manna was said to have healing properties and pilgrims came from far and wide to collect it.

The bones of Nicholas remained undisturbed in his tomb for over seven hundred years, but then, in the eleventh century, the Byzantine Empire lost control of the region to the non-Christian, Seljuk Turks. Using this as an excuse to "rescue" the bones of Saint Nicholas, sailors from the Italian city of Bari went to Myra in 1087, broke into Nicholas's tomb over the protests of the priest, and took at least some of the bones. When they returned home, the city of Bari constructed a new cathedral dedicated to Saint Nicholas in order to house these stolen bones. Soon after they built the cathedral, the new tomb also began to release manna.

About a decade later, during the First Crusade, a group of Venetian sailors also descended on Myra and supposedly stole the bones of Saint Nicholas that the sailors from Bari had left behind. These relics were brought back to Venice and stored in the church of San Nicolò al Lido. Although modern analysis of the bones held in the two cities suggests that they are from the same skeleton, Bari became, and remains, the most important pilgrimage site for those seeking the blessings of Saint Nicholas.

he tumbled into the sea. By the time his father realized what had happened, it was too late. The boy was gone. Broken-hearted, the nobleman sailed on to Myra.

When he arrived, the man went up to the tomb of Saint Nicholas, still intending to keep his promise, but, when he tried to place the second golden cup on the tomb, an unseen hand pushed him back and knocked him to the floor. The man got up, picked up the cup, and again tried to place it on the tomb. Again, an invisible hand pushed him back.

Just as the man began to despair, a miracle occurred. His son walked in, carrying the original golden cup. Crying tears of joy, the man embraced his son and asked him what had happened. The son explained that as soon as he had fallen over the side of the ship, Saint Nicholas had appeared, plucked him from the water, and brought him safe and sound to Myra. Then, giving thanks to both God and Saint Nicholas, the man took both golden cups and placed them on the tomb.

This man told his story to all who would listen, and the people began to realize that Saint Nicholas was still watching over them. He still came to rescue those at sea, and he still watched over and protected children.

THE PATRIARCH AND THE ICONS

Many years later, in Constantinople, a man named Theophanus had a dream that he should commission three icons, paintings of great holy men, and give them to the Patriarch, the man who oversaw all the bishops of the area. So Theophanus paid an artist to paint three beautiful icons: one of Jesus Christ, one of Saint Theotokos, and the final one of Saint Nicholas. When the icons were finished, Theophanus invited the Patriarch to dinner and presented the icons to him.

The Patriarch accepted the icons of Jesus and Saint Theotokos, but when he saw the icon of Saint Nicholas, he scowled.

"Saint Nicholas should not be put on icons," said the Patriarch. "His parents were mere peasants."

Saddened, Theophanus kept the icon of Saint Nicholas and put it up in his own house.

A few days later, the Patriarch was asked to visit the sick daughter of a man who lived out on an island. Boarding a small boat, the Patriarch was making for the island, when a tremendous storm rolled in. The rolling waves tossed the little boat from side to side and threw the Patriarch in the water. Struggling to keep his head above the waves, the gasping Patriarch called out to heaven.

"Oh great Saints, please save me!"

At that moment, Saint Nicholas appeared.

"Would you accept help from this peasants' son?" asked Nicholas with a grin.

"Forgive me, great Saint Nicholas. From today onward, I will celebrate your name!"

Saint Nicholas pulled the Patriarch out of the water and set him safely on land. Then he vanished.

When the Patriarch returned to Constantinople, he called on Theophanus and asked for the icon of Saint Nicholas. Theophanus happily gave it to him. The Patriarch had a new church built, dedicated to Saint Nicholas, and he put the icon in the place of honor.

This was just one of the many churches that were now dedicated to the life of Saint Nicholas, for he had become one of the most famous and popular of all the saints, and many people celebrated the day of his death, December 6, as a holy day.

THE COUPLE AND THE CARPET

There was an old couple who had celebrated Saint Nicholas's day every year for the whole of their long lives, but now both the man and woman were too old to work and they had no children to look after them. So, they slowly began to sell off all of their possessions in order to buy food. By the time the next Saint Nicholas's day came around, the only possession they had left was a faded carpet.

Then the woman said to her husband, "You had better take this carpet to market and see what money you can get for it, for it is all we have left. With the money, buy food for a feast so we may honor Saint Nicholas."

So the old man rolled up the carpet, hefted it onto his old shoulder, and walked slowly to the market place. As soon as he was there, he was approached by a tall and noble looking gentleman. The gentleman asked the old man how much money he wanted for the carpet. The man, not really sure how much it was worth, told the gentleman how much he had paid for it when it was new.

The gentleman smiled and offered him six pieces of gold, far more than it had ever been worth. The old man accepted the money with gratitude and gave the carpet to the gentleman.

When the old man turned around, he found that everyone in the market place was staring at him. They asked him, "Who were you talking to? And what happened to the carpet you were carrying?"

Confused, the old man turned around to look for the gentleman, but he had vanished into the crowded market. The old man just shrugged his shoulders, tucked the gold coins into his pouch, and went off to buy food for the feast.

A little while later, the old man's wife came out of their house and looked to see if her husband had returned. As she was standing there, a gentleman walked up carrying their old carpet. He smiled at the woman and placed the carpet before her.

"Your husband is an old friend of mine," said the gentleman. "He gave me this carpet at the market today. Could you please give it back to him?"

The woman looked down at the carpet and when she looked up the man had gone. A few minutes later, her husband walked up to the house and stared with astonishment at the carpet on the ground.

"How did that get there?" he asked.

"A man claiming to be your friend brought it. You were supposed to sell it."

"I did," said the man, and he showed his wife the gold coins.

Then the old man understood everything that had happened. "It was an old friend of ours," he whispered. "It was Saint Nicholas. This is his day, and he visited me in the market. That is why no one else could see him."

When others heard the story of the old couple, they too began to honor the feast of Saint Nicholas, and some even gave little presents to one another, in memory of the presents that Nicholas had given to people both during his life and after.

THE MONEYLENDER AND THE STAFF

As the traditions around Saint Nicholas and his feast day grew, people also remembered him as a man of justice. He was a man who always knew right from wrong and rewarded those who were truthful and fair, while chastising those who sought to take advantage of others.

One day, many centuries after the death of Nicholas, a desperate man came to a moneylender to ask for help. Although the man had nothing of value to offer for the money, he made a vow in the name of Saint Nicholas that he would repay all the money that was borrowed and more. Although the moneylender was not a Christian, he was impressed by the vow and loaned the man all of the money he needed.

Sometime later, the moneylender heard that the borrower had made a great deal of money using what he had borrowed, so he went to ask him to repay the loan. The borrower lied and said that he had already repaid the money. This angered the moneylender, and he called the borrower before the judges.

Before the borrower went to the court, he took his staff, hollowed out the inside, and filled it with money. When he finally arrived in court, he asked the moneylender to hold his staff while he spoke. Then, standing before the judges, and pointing to the moneylender holding the staff, he declared that he had given the moneylender all of the money he had owed and more. The judges could find no lie in the borrower's words, so they decided the case in his favor.

That afternoon, as the borrower walked home with his staff, he decided to take a nap on the side of the road. Unfortunately, as he slept, an out-of-control wagon came thundering down the road. It ran over the sleeping man and killed him. It also broke open the staff and spilled the money all about.

When word reached the moneylender of what had happened, he went out to see for himself. There amongst the gathered crowd, he saw the broken staff and the money, and he finally understood how the man could lie so convincingly in front of the judges. The crowd urged the moneylender to take the money that was rightfully his, but he would not touch it.

"This money has been cursed by Saint Nicholas, and I would not touch it without his blessing."

After he said those words, an old man with a white beard stepped out of the crowd. He bent down, touched the dead man's hand, and told him to rise up. The borrower opened his eyes, and, to the astonishment of the crowd, got to his feet. Then he turned to the moneylender and asked him to take the money which he owed to him, with his thanks, and the blessing of Saint Nicholas.

Then everyone there knew the name of the bearded man, but when they looked for him, he had vanished.

THE KIDNAPPED CHILD

And so the centuries passed, and as Christianity spread all over Europe, so did the stories of Saint Nicholas. His memory outlived the Roman Empire and all of the little kingdoms that came after it. In many places, his feast day became one of the most important holy days on the calendar, especially as it came so close to Christmas. In time, many people celebrated the feast of Saint Nicholas with big meals and parties, and nowhere celebrated quite as much as the city of Myra.

It was during one such celebration that pirates from Crete arrived and attacked the town. Along with terrifying the people, the pirates went to the Church of Saint Nicholas and stole all of its treasures.

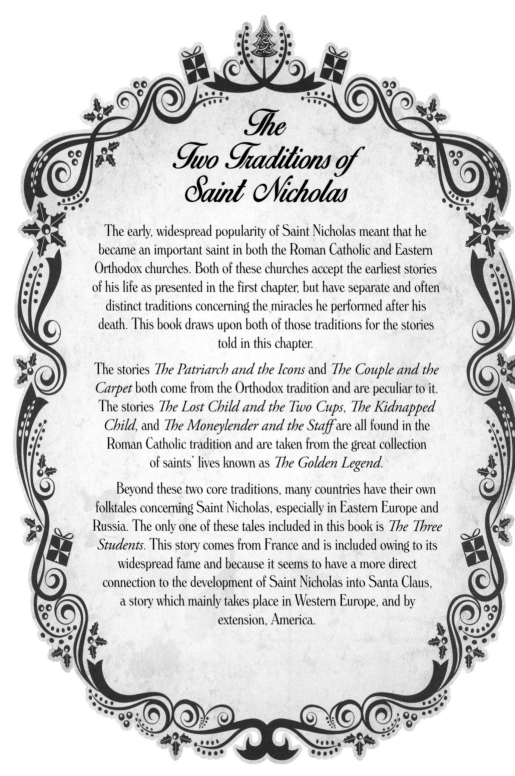

The Two Traditions of Saint Nicholas

The early, widespread popularity of Saint Nicholas meant that he became an important saint in both the Roman Catholic and Eastern Orthodox churches. Both of these churches accept the earliest stories of his life as presented in the first chapter, but have separate and often distinct traditions concerning the miracles he performed after his death. This book draws upon both of those traditions for the stories told in this chapter.

The stories *The Patriarch and the Icons* and *The Couple and the Carpet* both come from the Orthodox tradition and are peculiar to it. The stories *The Lost Child and the Two Cups*, *The Kidnapped Child*, and *The Moneylender and the Staff* are all found in the Roman Catholic tradition and are taken from the great collection of saints' lives known as *The Golden Legend*.

Beyond these two core traditions, many countries have their own folktales concerning Saint Nicholas, especially in Eastern Europe and Russia. The only one of these tales included in this book is *The Three Students*. This story comes from France and is included owing to its widespread fame and because it seems to have a more direct connection to the development of Saint Nicholas into Santa Claus, a story which mainly takes place in Western Europe, and by extension, America.

They took the silver candelabras, the carefully painted icons, and all of the golden chalices. As the pirates headed back to their boats with their stolen treasure, they grabbed hold of a young boy named Adeodatus and took him with them.

When the pirates returned to Crete, they sold Adeodatus as a slave to their king. Since the boy did not know the language, and thus could not understand anything that the king said in private, he used the boy as his cupbearer and kept him always by his side.

For a long and unhappy year, Adeodatus carried the king's cup and followed in silence wherever he went. Then, when the feast of Saint Nicholas came around again, the king caught Adeodatus crying.

"Why are you weeping?" said the king in the boy's own language.

"I'm thinking about my home and parents. There will be feasts and celebrations for today is the day of Saint Nicholas."

The king laughed. "Your Saint Nicholas can do as he likes, but you will never see your home again."

At that moment, a mighty wind tore across the island. It tore down the king's palace and sent everyone fleeing for safety. In the chaos, Saint Nicholas appeared, took the hand of Adeodatus, and bore him away.

In an instant, Adeodatus stood in front of his parents' house, still holding the king's golden cup. When he walked inside, he found his parents getting ready to celebrate the feast.

They rushed to embrace their son, and everyone gave thanks to the great saint who had once been their bishop.

THE THREE STUDENTS

As Saint Nicholas performed more and more miracles to help children, his name and his feast day became more associated with children than with any other group. There is, however, one story about Saint Nicholas helping children that is more famous than all the others. Some of the details have been lost, and not everyone agrees exactly how it happened, but essentially it concerns three young students who were on their way home.

The students had been traveling all day, and the sun had long gone down behind the hills. The students were tired and hungry and they decided to stop for the night. Just then, they saw an inn, with the glow of a warm fire flickering in the window. Happy to have found a place to rest, they went inside.

Everything was quiet inside the inn, except for the pop and crackle of the fire. No one else sat in the large common room. As the students wondered what to do, a door opened, and a large man came into the room. He was polishing a butcher's knife with a dirty rag.

"Are you the innkeeper?" asked one of the students. "We are hungry and would like a place to sleep."

"Have you got money?" asked the innkeeper.

All three students held up their full coin pouches so the innkeeper could see.

Then the man nodded and said, "Wait at the table, I'll bring you some food."

As the students relaxed by the fire, the innkeeper went to the kitchen where a pot of stew simmered over a cooking fire. Then he went to a dusty shelf and got down an old jar that had been hidden behind some others. The innkeeper poured a bunch of dark powder from the jar into the stew. Then he took three bowls, filled them to the top with the hot stew, and took them out to the students.

The students thanked the innkeeper and all three quickly devoured their meal. However, as soon as they had finished, they all got very sleepy and within minutes had fallen asleep at the table.

When the evil innkeeper saw that they were all asleep, he crept back into the room with his butcher's knife. He took the coin pouches from each of the students; then he chopped the children up into pieces with his knife. He gathered up the pieces of the students, and dumped them in a pickle barrel in his store room.

Later that night, as the innkeeper sat down to count the money he had stolen, there was a knock at his door. The innkeeper ignored it, but then the knock was heard again. Annoyed, he got up and opened the door, intending to tell whoever it was that the inn was closed. Instead, as he opened the door, his mouth fell open in surprise. There on his doorstep stood Saint Nicholas, dressed in the red and white robes of a bishop.

Saint Nicholas pushed the man aside and marched into the inn, heading straight back to the storeroom. The innkeeper followed behind, too terrified to get in his way. Saint Nicholas stopped in front of the pickle barrel where the innkeeper had hidden the bodies of the three students. He pulled the top off the barrel and looked at the murky brine within. Then holding a hand over the barrel, Saint Nicholas commanded the three students to get out.

One by one, the three students climbed out of the barrel, whole and alive once more. Seeing this, the innkeeper fell to the floor and begged Saint Nicholas for forgiveness. Saint Nicholas looked deep into the man's soul and could see that the man had truly changed. He granted him forgiveness, but made him vow that he would always help children in need and never accept any money for helping them.

The students, of course, told everyone what had happened to them, and once again Saint Nicholas became famous as the special saint who watched over children. The story proved so popular that it spread all over the country and in many places was even performed as a play on Saint Nicholas's day.

CHAPTER 3

The Gift Bringers

During the Middle Ages, Saint Nicholas became one of the most famous and most popular of all of the Catholic saints. By the end of the fifteenth century, hundreds of churches, chapels, monasteries, schools, and hospitals had been named in his honor. Many countries adopted him as their patron saint, including Greece, Germany, Belgium, Austria, Italy, and Switzerland, and nearly every other country in Europe had a least a couple of towns and cities who claimed Saint Nicholas as their patron. Although Nicholas had long been the special saint of sailors, he also became the patron of dozens of other groups because of the many miracles he had performed. This long and diverse list includes such odd groups as archers, barrel makers, butchers, embalmers, fire fighters, judges, military intelligence, orphans, pawnbrokers, prisoners, rag pickers, ribbon weavers, shoe shiners, teachers, and wine merchants. Yet, despite the many who claimed the special protection of Saint Nicholas, he became most famous for his role as a protector of children.

It was sometime during the Middle Ages, nobody knows exactly when, that Saint Nicholas began to make special visits to children on the eve of his saint's day, December 6th. During these visits he would leave little treats such as toys, sweets, or fruit on doorsteps. It is believed that he made the first of these visits in France, but soon he started traveling all over Western Europe, where children most strongly believed in him. In some countries he would climb through windows, in others he would slide down chimneys. Sometimes he would leave his gifts in shoes or stockings. In some countries, especially ones in the far north, he would ride a large white horse to help him in his nightly travels. In a few special places, he appeared in person to deliver gifts, dressed in the red and white robes of a bishop.

Although Saint Nicholas loved all children, he did not give presents to everyone. He only gave treats to those children who had been well behaved and said their prayers as their parents instructed. As in life, Nicholas could see into people's hearts and judge whether they had been good or if they were truly sorry for any bad things that they had done. If not, Nicholas would leave an empty shoe or stocking as a reminder for a child to try harder in the coming year.

As the years and decades passed, Saint Nicholas visited more and more places as more children heard of his visits and came to

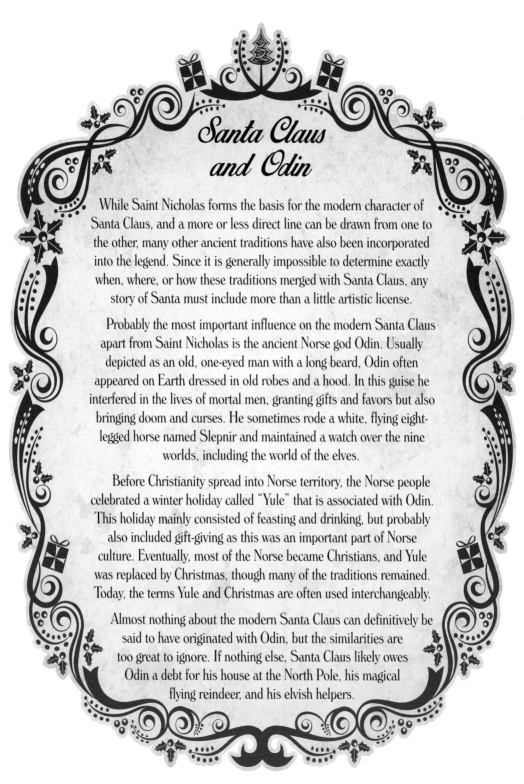

Santa Claus and Odin

While Saint Nicholas forms the basis for the modern character of Santa Claus, and a more or less direct line can be drawn from one to the other, many other ancient traditions have also been incorporated into the legend. Since it is generally impossible to determine exactly when, where, or how these traditions merged with Santa Claus, any story of Santa must include more than a little artistic license.

Probably the most important influence on the modern Santa Claus apart from Saint Nicholas is the ancient Norse god Odin. Usually depicted as an old, one-eyed man with a long beard, Odin often appeared on Earth dressed in old robes and a hood. In this guise he interfered in the lives of mortal men, granting gifts and favors but also bringing doom and curses. He sometimes rode a white, flying eight-legged horse named Slepnir and maintained a watch over the nine worlds, including the world of the elves.

Before Christianity spread into Norse territory, the Norse people celebrated a winter holiday called "Yule" that is associated with Odin. This holiday mainly consisted of feasting and drinking, but probably also included gift-giving as this was an important part of Norse culture. Eventually, most of the Norse became Christians, and Yule was replaced by Christmas, though many of the traditions remained. Today, the terms Yule and Christmas are often used interchangeably.

Almost nothing about the modern Santa Claus can definitively be said to have originated with Odin, but the similarities are too great to ignore. If nothing else, Santa Claus likely owes Odin a debt for his house at the North Pole, his magical flying reindeer, and his elvish helpers.

believe in him. Also, the celebrations around his visits became more and more elaborate, with towns and cities holding large festivals to celebrate his saint's day. These often included parades, dances, feasting, and drinking. Although most people enjoyed these celebrations, some people thought that they were beginning to get a little out of hand...

THE REFORMATION

In the early years of the sixteenth century, a German Catholic priest named Martin Luther wrote a long letter to his bishop calling for reforms in the church. Within weeks, copies of this letter had spread all over Germany and they became the rallying point for groups of reformers to band together and challenge the traditional practices of the Catholic Church. In the chaotic years that followed, this Reformation changed the way that large parts of Europe viewed religion. In many countries, the reformers threw out the Catholic Church and set up their own churches. These new "Protestant" churches still believed in God and Jesus, but they did not believe in the stories and the powers of the saints. They removed all the statues of saints from their churches and smashed stained-glass windows that showed pictures of their stories. They did not offer prayers to saints or ask for their protection.

As the Reformation grew and spread across Europe, many of the old traditions died away in some places, including the celebration of Saint Nicholas's day. Many of the reformers thought the idea of Saint Nicholas bringing presents to children was a silly fantasy that didn't fit with a true belief in God. So members of Protestant churches quit praying to the old bishop and stopped believing in the stories of all of his miracles. Saint Nicholas could not travel to places where people didn't believe in him, and so he stopped visiting.

KRAMPUS AND THE CHRISTMAS DEMONS

Not everything worked out as the reformers wanted. In many places the old religion and the belief in the saints were very popular, and the clash between the new and old religions caused confusion and even violence. Although Saint Nicholas continued to visit those places and those people who still believed in him, the chaos and fear caused by the religious fighting allowed other strange creatures to try to work against him. Many of these were very old demon-monsters that had stalked the world in ancient times. They had gone into hiding after the coming of Jesus, but now they saw a new opportunity to work mischief. Although Saint Nicholas did his best to protect children from these monsters, he didn't have the strength to completely stop them, especially when they went after children who had been naughty.

The most famous of these monsters was a demon called Krampus. Born in the Austrian Alps, Krampus was a large, hairy creature with cloven hooves, long goat horns, and a forked tongue. Every year, Krampus came down from the mountains on the eve of Saint Nicholas's Day to hunt after naughty children that he knew Saint Nicholas couldn't protect. He would stalk through the towns and villages, rattling his heavy iron chains. Over his shoulder, he carried an old sack. When Krampus found a child who had been exceptionally naughty, he would grab the child and stuff him or her in his sack. Some say that he took them home to eat them, others say he carried them off to hell. Either way, these children were never seen again.

For children who had only been a little bit bad, Saint Nicholas could still offer them some protection and would stop Krampus from carrying them off in his sack. However, for these children, Krampus carried a long thin branch, called a switch. When he caught children who had been a little naughty he would strike them with his switch and send them crying home to their parents.

Krampus was the most famous of these monsters, but he was not the only one. In parts of Germany a creature called Pelznickel also hunted misbehaving children. A bent and creepy old man, Pelznickel dressed in ragged furs and sometimes wore a mask. He also carried a long, painful switch that he used to punish naughty children on the night before Saint Nicholas's Day.

Another monster who took advantage of the situation was Knecht Ruprecht, a little man who wore furs and carried a long staff and a bag of ashes. He would rush around ahead of Saint Nicholas and see

which children could pray. If the children could pray, he left them for Saint Nicholas; if they could not, he would beat them with his sack of ashes.

These are just a few of the strange monsters that Saint Nicholas had to battle against; there were many more. Some he has managed to drive off for good, but others, like Krampus, are still occasionally seen today.

FATHER CHRISTMAS

In many countries that contained both Catholics and Protestants, Saint Nicholas adopted a new disguise in the hope of preventing arguments. In England, France, and Italy he became known as Father Christmas and moved his visits from his old saint's day of December 6 to Christmas Day. He also traded in his traditional bishop's robes for a selection of new outfits. Although Father Christmas still has Nicholas's long, white beard, he dresses in green or red robes, trimmed with white fur. Often these robes are a bit old and worn and he decorates them with little bits of holly or mistletoe. Sometimes he wears a floppy fur hat, other times he wears a hood.

In the early years of Father Christmas, Nicholas changed his focus from giving gifts to children to promoting peace and good cheer in the Christmas season in the hopes of healing some of the damage done by all of the religious fighting. In those days he performed little miracles of human kindness and promoted generosity. Although there were still some Protestants who wanted to get rid of all of the trappings of Christmas, including

Father Christmas, they were generally in the minority, and Saint Nicholas seems to have succeeded in more places than he failed. In England, he became such a popular figure that Charles Dickens included him in his book *A Christmas Carol*, renaming him "The Ghost of Christmas Present" and making him a jovial giant.

Eventually, as the various Christian churches learned to live with one another, the figure of Father Christmas would slowly merge with Saint Nicholas's more famous incarnation as Santa Claus and the two would basically become different names for the same man. That, however, is getting slightly ahead of the story.

SINTERKLAAS

For many centuries, the small country of the Netherlands had celebrated the visits of Sinterklaas (their name for Saint Nicholas) with great feasts and parades. However, during the Reformation, the country essentially split in half along religious lines. In the north, the Protestants took over and banned the celebration of Sinterklaas. In the Catholic south, the tradition continued.

In the south, Sinterklaas would arrive in the country by boat sometime in November, and spend the next few weeks, until December 6, touring the country, spreading good cheer, and giving out small gifts and presents to the children. He dressed like a bishop with his red and white robes, his tall hat, and his crozier (his special bishop's staff). He also carried a large book, which contained the names of all the children and included notes on which ones had been good and which ones had been naughty.

In his visits to the Netherlands, Sinterklaas also brought along a helper named Zwarte Piet, a young Ethiopian boy that Sinterklaas had rescued from slavery. Zwarte Piet assisted Sinterklaas by carrying his sack full of presents and tossing out small candies and chocolates to the children. He also sometimes helped guide

The Christkind

In many Protestant countries, the religious authorities encouraged people to replace Saint Nicholas with the "Christ-child," meaning the young Jesus. This began in Germany, where he was called the Christkind, but quickly spread to many Protestant parts of Central and Western Europe. Instead of giving gifts on Saint Nicholas's day, the celebrations were moved to Christmas, the day of Jesus's birth.

In an odd twist, the tradition of the Christkind slowly died out in most Protestant countries during the nineteenth century as a more secular version of Saint Nicholas rose in popularity. Instead, the Christkind became popular in more Catholic countries, and remains the main gift bringer in many Catholic countries in Latin America.

Some early European settlers in America brought the tradition of the Christkind with them, under the name of Kris Kringle. However, this tradition was eventually subsumed into the more popular American Christmas legend, and these days Kris Kringle has become yet another name for Santa Claus.

Sinterklaas's ship and was even known to climb down chimneys and leave presents.

The Netherlands was lucky, in that it was one of the few countries that Saint Nicholas consistently visited for more than one day a year. In fact, Sinterklaas still visits the Netherlands every year for a few weeks, and these days he once again visits the whole country, not just the south. Unlike in many other European countries,

the identity of Sinterklaas has remained distinct from Santa Claus. This is especially interesting because it is in his form as Sinterklaas that Saint Nicholas seems to have first visited the New World, and from Sinterklaas that he developed his more common modern name of Santa Claus.

CHAPTER 4

Santa Claus

In 1625, Dutch settlers founded the colony of New Amsterdam on the island of Manhattan. Although these early settlers were Protestant, and probably did not believe in Saint Nicholas, they still played an important part in his first visits to the New World as will be seen. In 1666, the British took control of the colony, and renamed it New York. There aren't many historical records from this time, but there are a few clues, such as old nursery rhymes, that Saint Nicholas did make a few visits to the New World in the next one hundred years. But they must have been few and far between, because most of Colonial America was still strictly Protestant.

The situation changed after the American Revolution ended in 1783. The new American government made

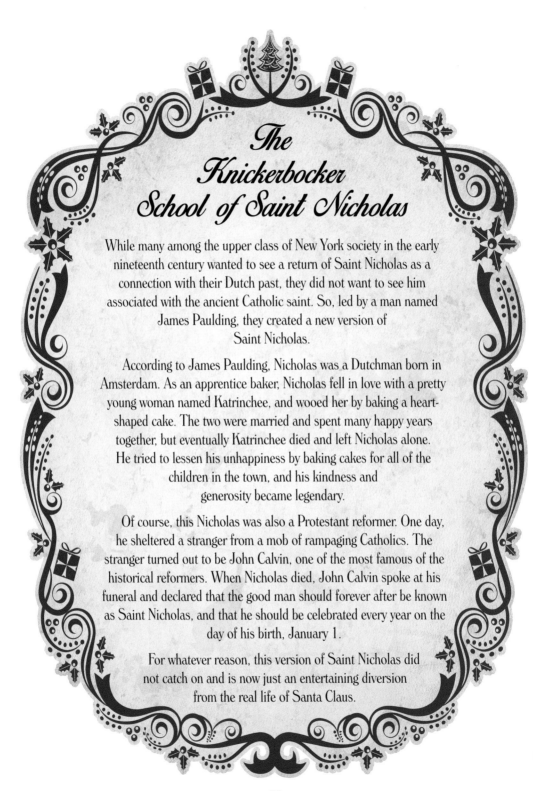

The Knickerbocker School of Saint Nicholas

While many among the upper class of New York society in the early nineteenth century wanted to see a return of Saint Nicholas as a connection with their Dutch past, they did not want to see him associated with the ancient Catholic saint. So, led by a man named James Paulding, they created a new version of Saint Nicholas.

According to James Paulding, Nicholas was a Dutchman born in Amsterdam. As an apprentice baker, Nicholas fell in love with a pretty young woman named Katrinchee, and wooed her by baking a heart-shaped cake. The two were married and spent many happy years together, but eventually Katrinchee died and left Nicholas alone. He tried to lessen his unhappiness by baking cakes for all of the children in the town, and his kindness and generosity became legendary.

Of course, this Nicholas was also a Protestant reformer. One day, he sheltered a stranger from a mob of rampaging Catholics. The stranger turned out to be John Calvin, one of the most famous of the historical reformers. When Nicholas died, John Calvin spoke at his funeral and declared that the good man should forever after be known as Saint Nicholas, and that he should be celebrated every year on the day of his birth, January 1.

For whatever reason, this version of Saint Nicholas did not catch on and is now just an entertaining diversion from the real life of Santa Claus.

the country free for the followers of all religions, and floods of immigrants of various beliefs came to the country. Also, since the British were not very popular in the years following the revolution, people began to take more of an interest in the early Dutch settlers who had founded New York. One such person was the writer Washington Irving, who would later become famous for writing such stories as *The Legend of Sleepy Hollow* and *Rip Van Winkle*.

DIEDRICH KNICKERBOCKER

In 1809, Washington Irving released a book called *A History of New-York from the Beginning of the World to the End of the Dutch Dynasty*, supposedly written by the Dutch historian Diedrich Knickerbocker. In the book, Irving made a lot of fanciful claims. He said that the early Dutch settlers adopted Saint Nicholas as their patron saint and always celebrated his saint's day. He also claimed that a carven image of Saint Nicholas had been on the front of the ship that had brought the first Dutch settlers to the new world.

There is no reason to believe that anything Washington Irving said about Saint Nicholas in his book was true, but that did not matter. The book was a huge success and read all over America. By the very next year, more people were writing about Saint Nicholas, especially in New York. In those early days of America, when the English language was less formalized than it is now, and when people of many different cultures and languages were all coming into the country at once, Saint Nicholas was often called by strange names. Some people used the old Dutch name, Sinterklaas.

Sometimes it was abbreviated, and became something like St. a Claus. In 1810, one New York newspaper printed a poem about "Santce Claus."

So there was still a debate about his name and how it should be spelled, but, more importantly, in the early decades of the nineteenth century, the belief in Saint Nicholas grew in America. Once more the old Bishop of Myra came to the people who believed in him to bring gifts and to spread joy.

THE NIGHT BEFORE CHRISTMAS

By the early 1820s numerous people across America had reported seeing good Saint Nicholas and many of these accounts appeared in print. In 1821, a book called *The Children's Friend* became the first to report seeing "Santeclaus" traveling through the air in a sleigh pulled by a reindeer. It also included a little picture of Santa Claus in his sleigh, although he looks very little like the Santa Claus we know today.

Just one year later, a New York Professor named Clement Clarke Moore reported the most famous sighting of Saint Nicholas in American history. He wrote it down in a poem, but did nothing with it. Luckily, a friend sent a copy of the poem to a newspaper and it was published under the title *An Account of a Visit from Saint Nicholas*. These days it is better known as *'Twas the Night Before Christmas*, and it remains one of the most popular and widely read poems in American history. It is such an important account of the new way in which Saint Nicholas visited his believers in America that the whole poem is included here.

'Twas the night before Christmas, when all thro' the house

Not a creature was stirring, not even a mouse;

The stockings were hung by the chimney with care,

In hopes that St. Nicholas soon would be there;

The children were nestled all snug in their beds,

While visions of sugar plums danc'd in their heads,

And Mama in her 'kerchief, and I in my cap,

Had just settled our brains for a long winter's nap –

When out on the lawn there arose such a clatter,

I sprang from the bed to see what was the matter.

Away to the window I flew like a flash,

Tore open the shutters, and threw up the sash.

The moon on the breast of the new fallen snow,

Gave the luster of mid-day to objects below;

When, what to my wondering eyes should appear,

But a miniature sleigh, and eight tiny reindeer,

With a little old driver, so lively and quick,

I knew in a moment it must be St. Nick.

More rapid than eagles his coursers they came,

And he whistled, and shouted, and call'd them by name:

"Now! Dasher, now! Dancer, now! Prancer and Vixen,

"On! Comet, on! Cupid, on! Dunder and Blixem;

"To the top of the porch! To the top of the wall!

"Now dash away! Dash away! Dash away all!"

As dry leaves that before the wild hurricane fly,

When they meet with an obstacle, mount to the sky;

So up to the house-top the coursers they flew,

With the sleigh full of toys – and St. Nicholas too:

And then in a twinkling, I heard on the roof

The prancing and pawing of each little hoof.

As I drew in my head, and was turning around,

Down the chimney St. Nicholas came with a bound:

He was dress'd all in fur, from his head to his foot,

And his clothes were all tarnish'd with ashes and soot;

A bundle of toys was flung on his back,

And he look'd like a peddler just opening his pack:

His eyes – how they twinkled! His dimples: how merry,

His cheeks were like roses, his nose like a cherry;

His droll little mouth was drawn up like a bow,

And the beard of his chin was as white as the snow;

The stump of a pipe he held tight in his teeth,

And the smoke it encircled his head like a wreath.

He had a broad face, and a little round belly

That shook when he laugh'd, like a bowl full of jelly:

He was chubby and plump, a right jolly old elf,

And I laugh'd when I saw him in spite of myself;

A wink of his eye and a twist of his head

Soon gave me to know I had nothing to dread.

He spoke not a word, but went straight to his work,

And fill'd all the stockings; then turn'd with a jerk,

And laying his finger aside of his nose

And giving a nod, up the chimney he rose.

He sprung to his sleigh, to his team gave a whistle,

And away they all flew, like the down of a thistle:

But I heard him exclaim, ere he drove out of sight –

Happy Christmas to all, and to all a good night.

In later years, it would be discovered that Clement Clarke Moore had misheard the names of the last two reindeer. These are actually "Donner" and "Blixen." Later printings of the poem have corrected this mistake, but in most other aspects Moore wrote the first clear description of Saint Nicholas's modern American form of Santa Claus, even if Moore himself didn't use the name.

THE NORTH POLE

For the first thousand years or more after his death, Saint Nicholas lived in Heaven, occasionally leaving to help those who called upon him for assistance. This situation worked fine when he spent most of his time helping sailors or children out of dangerous situations. However, when Nicholas began to make regular visits to lots of people on the same night, either on his saint's day or on Christmas Eve, to deliver treats and presents, he needed to establish a workshop. Since there is no need for candy or presents in Heaven, such things need to be made on earth.

The first workshop that Saint Nicholas built on Earth seems to have been somewhere in Spain. From there he could take his boat up to the Netherlands as Sinterklaas and then he could ride his flying horse around the rest of Europe. It is almost certain that this Spanish workshop still exists, and is still used for his trips to the Netherlands, but it is no longer his main headquarters.

Sometime later, Saint Nicholas set up a new workshop in Iceland, and soon thereafter moved it to Lapland in northern Finland. Why he chose this location is unknown, but it appears to be where he acquired his magical sleigh and reindeer. It is also probably where he first recruited the elves to work in his workshop. Elves have been known to inhabit parts of Northern Europe for thousands of years, and are mentioned in many ancient stories. They are much less common today, and have always been shy around humans, which is why we don't see them very often. Saint Nicholas probably recruited them because of their magical skills at making objects like toys and decorations.

The Lapland workshop allowed Saint Nicholas to greatly expand his operations and visit more people on a single night. This became very important as more and more people called upon his visits on Christmas Eve and less on Saint Nicholas's Day, and because he now had to visit both Europe and America in one night.

By the mid-nineteenth century, even this Lapland headquarters was not big enough. Thanks to Clement Clarke Moore's poem, the book *A Christmas Carol* by Charles Dickens, and numerous other writings, Saint Nicholas and the celebration of Christmas had grown so popular that his workshop and elves were stretched

to the limit. He needed to move someplace where he could build an even bigger headquarters, somewhere that would give him lots of room to expand in the future. He also wanted somewhere quiet and remote where he and his shy elves could devote themselves to their work without being disturbed. So, sometime in the second half of the nineteenth century, Santa Claus built a new workshop at the North Pole.

THOMAS NAST

Thomas Nast was a German-born American, who made his living drawing political cartoons for newspapers. He is also thought to be the first person to visit Santa Claus in the North Pole. We don't know exactly when, or even how, Thomas Nast made the trip, but

Coca-Cola and Santa Claus

Many people now believe that the modern image of Santa Claus was invented by Coca-Cola as part of their annual Christmas advertising campaign that started in the 1930s. This is not the case. All of the elements that appeared in Haddon Hubbard Sundblom's famous paintings of Santa Claus drinking a Coke already existed. In fact, most can be found in the drawings of Thomas Nast.

However, previous to those Coke adverts, there had been lots of different versions and ideas about what Santa Claus looked like. Because the Coca-Cola adverts were so widespread and seen by virtually everyone in American at some point during the 1930s, 40s, 50s, and 60s, it established the version of Santa Claus that Sundblom chose to illustrate as *the* version, and all of the other different looks of Saint Nicholas slowly died out.

in 1865 he published a drawing called *Santa Claus and His Works*. This cartoon showed Santa Claus doing all kinds of different activities, including working in his workshop, flying in his sleigh, making toys in his workshop, and even checking over a huge book of names where he recorded which children had been naughty and which had been nice.

Over the next couple of decades, Thomas Nast would draw many more pictures of Santa Claus and the things he saw at the North Pole. He never drew any elves – they were probably too shy to come out while he was there – but he created many wonderful drawings of Santa Claus making his rounds on Christmas Eve, dressed in his red fur coat, with its wide black belt. He showed him hard at work at his desk, reading all of the letters that children had sent him. Some people even believe that Thomas Nast spent one Christmas Eve traveling with Santa in his sleigh, because he drew many images of Santa going down chimneys, filling stockings with goodies, and even visiting a few little children who had stayed up past their bedtime.

Thomas Nast never spoke about visiting with Santa Claus, but in 1889, many of his drawings of Santa were collected in a book entitled *Thomas Nast's Christmas Drawings for the Human Race*. It is one of the most important books about Santa Claus, and for many Americans it was the first time that they had seen what Saint Nicholas actually looked like in those days.

MRS. CLAUS

One of the greatest mysteries that still surrounds Santa Claus is his wife, generally known as Mrs. Claus. She first appears in the middle of the nineteenth century, when she is mentioned in several stories and newspaper articles. She does not, however, appear in any of Thomas Nast's drawings. This has led to the belief that Nast actually visited the North Pole sometime in the 1850s and that Santa Claus probably got married a short time after that.

We know almost nothing about Mrs. Claus. There is no mention, or even hint, of a wife in the ancient stories of Saint Nicholas, nor even those of the Middle Ages. This makes sense. Saint Nicholas almost certainly would not have considered marriage until he had established a permanent home back on earth, which didn't occur until he moved to the North Pole.

We know very few facts about Mrs. Claus beyond her general appearance as a kindly, round-faced and rosy-cheeked, gray-haired woman. We are not even sure of her first name. In various places she has been called Martha, Mary, Louise, Layla, and a whole host of stranger names. It seems that most people are just guessing.

The little that we can say for certain comes from later drawings or paintings of artists who claim to have visited the North Pole. In these, we often see Mrs. Claus baking cookies and other Christmas treats. These seem to be both for children on Christmas Eve, and also for Santa and the elves while they are working. It also appears that Mrs. Claus is in charge of running the household, keeping things clean and making sure that all of Santa Claus's various tools and what-nots are where he needs them. Apparently,

Santa has become a little absent-minded these days, but Mrs. Claus always checks behind him to make sure that no child gets missed on Christmas Day.

It is also widely believed that Mrs. Claus is responsible for Santa Claus giving up smoking. During the early days of American history, Santa became fond of smoking a pipe, and later is sometimes seen with cigarettes. These days, he has clearly kicked the habit so as not to encourage any children to be attracted to tobacco.

RUDOLPH THE RED-NOSED REINDEER

After establishing himself at the North Pole, Santa, Mrs. Claus and the elves have slowly expanded their operations as more and more people around the world have come to believe in Old Saint Nick and called upon him to visit on Christmas Eve. For the most part, this expansion has gone unnoticed by most of the world. The news only tends to report on Santa Claus's activities in the days leading up to Christmas, and even then it usually only reports some major change to his operations. The last such big event occurred in 1939, when Rudolph, the famous red-nosed reindeer, was added to the team.

It was in the dark years before and during World War II that a series of especially bad winters hit around the North Pole. The constant snowstorms made it almost impossible for

Santa to see when flying his sleigh. He considered canceling his Christmas Eve visits. Then, just when he had almost given up, he discovered Rudolph. This young reindeer had endured a tough childhood, having been constantly bullied because of his glowing, red nose, but Santa recognized Rudolph's nose as a gift from God. Santa asked Rudolph to join the team that pulled his sleigh, so that the light from his red nose could help guide the way through the storms.

The story of Rudolph was first reported in a poem by Robert Lewis May, which appeared in a flyer given away by the Montgomery Ward department store. However, most people learned about Rudolph when the story was put to music and became a hit for the famous singing cowboy, Gene Autry.

Rudolph led Santa's reindeer team all through World War II and for at least a decade afterward. Because of this, he has become the most famous of all of Santa's reindeer. It appears that Rudolph retired from duty sometime in the 1970s or 80s, but still makes occasional trips with the team.

Yes, Virginia, There is a Santa Claus

Although Santa Claus is just the modern name for Saint Nicholas, the kindly bishop who served in Myra over 1,700 years ago, he is no longer seen as a purely Christian figure. Instead, he has become a champion of the Christmas season, a bringer of joy and good cheer who can be loved and called upon by people of any religion and any culture.

Over the last one hundred years, many people have claimed to have seen Santa Claus, interviewed him, visited him in the North Pole, and even convinced him to appear in movies and on television. It can be very difficult to figure out which of these people are telling the truth and which are just seeking attention. Unfortunately, because of the confusion created by all of these conflicting accounts, there is a rising belief in some places that Santa Claus does not exist, that he is just a story made up by parents to make their children smile.

Probably the best response to this claim was made over one hundred years ago, in the New York *Sun* newspaper. In 1897, eight-year-old Virginia O'Hanlon wrote a letter to the newspaper, saying:

> Dear Editor:
>
> I am 8 years old. Some of my little friends say there is no Santa Claus. Papa says, "If you see it in The Sun it's so." Please tell me the truth; is there a Santa Claus?

This letter was answered in the following editorial by the Francis Pharcellus Church, and for many people he provided the last word on the subject.

VIRGINIA, your little friends are wrong. They have been affected by the skepticism of a skeptical age. They do not believe except they see. They think that nothing can be which is not comprehensible by their little minds. All minds, Virginia, whether they be men's or children's, are little. In this great universe of ours man is a mere insect, an ant, in his intellect, as compared with the boundless world about him, as measured by the intelligence capable of grasping the whole of truth and knowledge.

Yes, VIRGINIA, there is a Santa Claus. He exists as certainly as love and generosity and devotion exist, and you know that they abound and give to your life its highest beauty and joy. Alas! how dreary would be the world if there were no Santa Claus. It would be as dreary as if there were no VIRGINIAS. There would be no childlike faith then, no poetry, no romance to make tolerable this existence. We should have no enjoyment, except in sense and sight. The eternal light with which childhood fills the world would be extinguished.

Not believe in Santa Claus! You might as well not believe in fairies! You might get your papa to hire men to watch in all the chimneys on Christmas Eve to catch Santa Claus, but even if they did not see Santa Claus coming down, what would that prove? Nobody sees Santa Claus, but that is no sign that there is no Santa Claus. The most real things in the world are those that neither children nor men can see. Did you ever see fairies dancing on the lawn? Of course not, but that's no proof that they are not there. Nobody can conceive or imagine all the wonders there are unseen and unseeable in the world.

You may tear apart the baby's rattle and see what makes the noise inside, but there is a veil covering the unseen world which not the strongest

man, nor even the united strength of all the strongest men that ever lived, could tear apart. Only faith, fancy, poetry, love, romance, can push aside that curtain and view and picture the supernal beauty and glory beyond. Is it all real? Ah, VIRGINIA, in all this world there is nothing else real and abiding.

No Santa Claus! Thank God! he lives, and he lives forever. A thousand years from now, Virginia, nay, ten times ten thousand years from now, he will continue to make glad the heart of childhood.

Sources

Historically, Saint Nicholas, Bishop of Myra, remains a controversial figure. He left behind no writings of his own, and there are no contemporary documents that mention his name. In fact, even the dates of his life cannot be backed up with any firm evidence.

On the other hand, only a short time after the period in which he lived, a large number of churches dedicated to Saint Nicholas were built. Also, around that time, "Nicholas" became a much more common name, where before it had been virtually unknown.

The first full *Life of St. Nicholas* that has survived was written around AD 700 by Michael the Archimandrite. Although no full translation of this work has ever been published in English, the author is indebted to his brother-in-law, Ian Gerdon, who provided a working translation to help with the preparation of this book. Although Michael's *Life of St. Nicholas* is a dense piece, filled with biblical quotes and obscure theological detail, it is the oldest source for many of the Saint Nicholas stories.

The stories of Saint Nicholas first became popular in written form in the great collection of saint stories known as *The Golden Legend* written in the thirteenth century by Jacobus de Voragine, the Archbishop of Genoa. It is these versions of the Saint Nicholas stories that are most common in Western Europe and America.

For those wishing to learn more about the historical Saint Nicholas and the academic debates that have gone on around him, I suggest reading *The Saint who would be Santa Claus: The True Life and Trials of Nicholas of Myra* by Adam C. English.

For those more interested in the modern version of Santa Claus and his development and growth in American society, I suggest *Santa Claus: A Biography* by Gerry Bowler.

Finally, I would like to thank my own parents who first taught me to believe in Santa Claus, who helped me write letters to him when I was young, and who ensured that Christmas was a magical time.

AUTHORS

Joseph A. McCullough is the author of numerous books including *A Pocket History of Ireland* and *Dragonslayers: From Beowulf to St. George*. In addition, his fantasy short stories have appeared in various books and magazines such as *Black Gate, Lords of Swords,* and *Adventure Mystery Tales*. He is a lifelong Santa Claus fan and caught a brief glimpse of the gift-bringer on Christmas Eve when he was eight.

ILLUSTRATOR

Peter Dennis was born in 1950. Inspired by contemporary magazines such as *Look and Learn,* he studied illustration at Liverpool Art College. Peter has since contributed to hundreds of books, predominantly on historical subjects, including many Osprey titles. Based in Nottinghamshire, UK, he will neither confirm nor deny that he has actually visited Santa's workshop in the North Pole.